The Lost Chronicle

Also by Polarbear

The Lost Chronicle 2004–2009

POLARBEAR

BLOOMSBURY POETRY

LONDON · OXFORD · NEW YORK · NEW DELHI · SYDNEY

BLOOSMBURY POETRY
Bloomsbury Publishing Plc
50 Bedford Square, London, WC1B 3DP, UK
29 Earlsfort Terrace, Dublin 2, Ireland

BLOOMSBURY, BLOOMSBURY POETRY and the Diana logo are
trademarks of Bloomsbury Publishing Plc

First published in Great Britain 2022

Copyright © Steven Camden, 2022

Steven Camden has asserted his right under the Copyright, Designs and
Patents Act, 1988, to be identified as Author of this work

For legal purposes the Acknowledgements on p. 177
constitute an extension of this copyright page

A catalogue record for this book is available from the British Library

ISBN: HB: 978-1-5266-4845-7; eBook: 978-1-5266-4846-4;
ePDF: 978-1-5266-4844-0

2 4 6 8 10 9 7 5 3 1

Typeset by Laura Jones
Printed and bound in Great Britain by
CPI Group (UK) Ltd, Croydon CR0 4YY

To find out more about our authors and books
visit www.bloomsbury.com and sign up for our newsletters

Mom
for your love and the space to try
thank you

BETWEEN 2004 AND 2009 I USED MY MOUTH TO
CREATE THE FOLLOWING PIECES TO BE SPOKEN AT GIGS

I GOT TO TRAVEL THE WORLD SPEAKING THEM

THIS IS THE FIRST TIME THEY HAVE BEEN WRITTEN
DOWN AND COLLECTED

THEY WERE MADE TO LIVE IN THE MOUTH

'Is he still a fly guy clappin' if nobody ain't hear it?
And can they testify from inner spirit?'

—MF DOOM, 'Accordion', Madvillainy (2004)

HEARTBURN

Where I come from   it rains a lot and
grown men still get called by their
playground nicknames a lot
day to day
it don't change   a lot and if
you wanna leave
they think you're strange

we buy Guinness and black
with loose change a lot
       don't get paid a lot
make afternoon visits to overgrown graves a lot
and if you leave and   come back
they say you've
changed

and that's my city
my city ain't pretty but I love it
you see me
I love my city
my city ain't pretty but it's home

I make a 4/4 beat when I'm yawning
four in the morning   all-night garage
Rizla and milk   cup of tea to fix
damage
born into more than I can manage
same old adage
same old man

moans 'bout home   won't roam further   the burden
   of marriage
a cross to carry
eat sleep breathe is a reason
to grieve
the uneven
each season don't seem to please
these demons
geezers speak evil   locked into pubs
whilst   back home
wives raise lives

Russian-doll offspring   popping out
every twenty years beers raised
to the old ones
                 dropping off

temper the cocktails Molotov
heartburn cars turn silent
seen in the corner of   right eye
tonight   I might die
tonight   I might try
flying to a place where
your dreams   aren't poison
and hopes are
a lifeline
cos it feels like the right time

but I'm anchored to wankers
filled up with passed-down anger
heavy enough to sink tankers

skinheads skank hard to Madness
hooligan Zulus
        booze to prove
        mantras
one lone frontman
                        no backing dancers
no second chances
                        no hidden answers

and I still feel the question
burn in my gut
can I push further   get out of a rut?
Can I make movements now?
Gotta make movements now
Gotta make movements
                        how?

So
I move down south
to *that London*

press my cards
to the left of my chest
where my heart is

one hundred and one parties
one hundred and one wannabe artists
chat fart hardest
my flat's my own TARDIS
stay sane   asking myself the quo vadis
old me?

Just a carcass
left by the side of the road got thrown
with no
harness

I'm not a martyr
I don't wanna die face down
in a pile of starving try-harders

Jason
trying to put nauts to my argos
cheques for the father
who grafted his arse off proper
won't come and go in one breath   like poppers
won't be forgotten
                    whatever
                    way more Hellboy   way less

Del Boy Trotter

show-stopper
golden flow proper
but it don't matter without   studio backing
indie film star just
budget that's lacking
summer jobs packing   labouring daily
never had the arrogance of 'fuck you, pay me'
but the seed develops when
I have to stand in line
behind
so-called name-game veterans

Why can't you just call a spade a spade mate?
If you're lame then you're lame
Do one!

my city taught me that
when I was on the brink of forgetting what's real
my city brought me back
      I'm just an ordinary chap
just so happens
I've a talent for reporting it back
and, oh yeah, *'Do one'*?
that's ours too
get your own one   softy

and that's my city in me
gold-plating my bones
      breathing its two-pence piece
every single time I speak

SAGAT

Since the date
nineteenth of the fifth
nineteen eighty-eight
I've been seeking that sweet state
where I permanently feel
great
from a clean slate to
splattered
        with colour

I think back to me on Nintendo
battering Sagat
while sat
        happily nyammin' a bulla
head full of dreams
cool stuff to come in my teens
I played for four football teams
turn-ups on all my jeans
        it all seemed
        to make sense
Saturdays I'd get a hundred pence
and most weekends it got spent
on penny sweets but
now and again
I'd fight the sugar rush   buy a 7" single
and running home
to put it on
my stomach would start to tingle

looking back now
the feeling seems so primal
so much pleasure from each circle of black vinyl
and time'll tell you
my passion only increased
every beautiful tune a feast and I went up
for thirds at least
my height rose like yeast and by the time I hit thirteen
I was like some kind of
      head-nod obsessed musical beast

MJ
the Roses
Aretha
Kate Bush
I took a job cleaning cars to keep
my musical plate flush
I didn't make much but
a new album was enough to
keep me buzzed
till the next week
my decisions became tough   see

the money I made
only let me pay for one
but when
I'd get down the shop there were
so many to choose from
Hendrix
Soul II Soul
Stevie Wonder
the Clash

I wanted them all so badly but
I was holding limited cash

so one day I grabbed a couple
and made a dash for the door
but the hippy dude jumped over
the counter fast and tackled me to the floor
            feeling so stupid
I cried and tried
to explain myself
he must've seen
something in my eyes
and gave me a job
stacking the shelves   and
although my monetary wealth didn't
really increase
I was as rich as I'd ever been
all I'd needed was the release

            we used to sit and talk all day
discuss the latest tracks
he'd let me take records home
as long as I promised to bring them back

I was learning a craft

understanding musical orders
then one day we got a release in
called *Midnight Marauders*

            I put it on

and something spoke
to my bones
my body got warm
young ears focused
drums and vocal tones

and that was it
                    hip-hop had me

and if you'd have asked me then
I would've agreed
to have that album engraved
on my brain gladly

obsessed madly
I walked home into the night
feeling the first fresh thought
of talking into a mic

ALEXANDER THE GRAPE

Him:

There's a photo
in one of Nan's old albums
of a boy
aged about three
spreadeagled on a bed
late afternoon light
brown velour jumpsuit and golden curls
everyone says that it's you
Steven
the good boy resting on soft cotton
even our mothers say so
but I guess
we see what we want to

I haven't been home
in a while
walked up those narrow stairs
smelled the coconut
and laughter
felt the thin grey carpet
under my feet
reached up to the top of her old wardrobe and
taken down that book of dusty leather
but I still see the picture

I see that boy through rain
and the stares of strangers

through nights
dark as the shelter
between buildings
and the cold sounds
a town makes
when people go to their homes

I'm quietly chasing dragons
but I still recognise my own face.

Me:

It's Thursday
the alarm goes
my arm knows its role

moves slowly
over snooze and delivers a calm blow

my twenty-year-old body
feels cold
broken morning after
false laughter
and somebody else's money

it's not funny
I've got an exam in ten minutes
but my stomach still hums
from overproof rum,
a shared gram and
five Guinness

'Every man should know his limits,'
Grandad said
but right now   all I know
is I don't know
my own mind
or any of the twisted things in it

8.50
I swiftly roll a nifty joint
in the vain hope
it'll help my brain cope
and mentally lift me
then it   hits me
that same tamed feeling of guilt
this whole charade
I've built means
I'm forever swimming in spilt milk and
the bits that filter
back home
are written in rose-tinted script saying
golden boy Steven is living and breathing
education driven to
achieving a gleaming degree
please
they tried to kick me off the course four times
and would have too
if I hadn't laid on sob stories
about worries and family strife
so
this is my life
a string of debt
self-abuse and lies   yet

it's strange how
you never suspect
sat round the table
at Christmas

the picture painted
with a tainted brush
must be protected
at all costs
my head throbs in that same spot
it does most days
the toast stays down too long
I pray
that the day stops
up pops the toast   it's black
in drops the post
promotional flyers
liars hoping I'll vote
crap
I scrape my bread
shake my head
scoop up the letters
intent on heading
straight back to bed
then
I see it
handwritten in ink and
I'm thinking
please let there be money for drinking
              see
I know Nan's writing
and any post from home

ignites a childish hope
for a folded note inside it
sent for provisions
and to subsidise
a crude student diet
my mind   quietly   wanders
through ways of spending
a crisp twenty   and they
all revolve around me
making a bottle empty
so I gently
              turn the envelope
and tear it open

a folded piece of A4

you're joking

still
I know I don't deserve it
and there's some kinda karmic
lesson here
I just don't wanna learn it
the burning
smell from my toast
brings me back with a thud
I was starting to feel better
now this letter's a dud
I sit on the stairs and read

Dear Steven,
I hope you've got everything you need

please tell me if there's anything I can do to help
I hope you're looking after yourself
healthy body healthy mind
and are you finding time to relax
with all the stress of exams
and moving out of the flat?

and at that exact point
I try to transmit
a telepathic message back home
that I'm doing jack shit
I haven't picked up a book
in nine months
and today I missed my second exam
cos last night I was quite drunk
and I'm sorry, Nan   I really am
I don't even know why I'm here
nearly three years
four scars
forged report cards
probably a million drinks downed and
at this point
tears would be worthless
so I just carry on breathing
and reading
not needing a purpose
then just when I think that you're done
you tell me Aaron's in trouble again
and it's to do
with the drugs

Him:

I remember
you made a joke machine
an overturned cardboard box
one slot – coins in   jokes out
you sat inside scribbling
on scraps of paper
you only knew one
What's purple and wants to rule the world?

it was my job
to find money and
get people to pay
two pence for the best joke
they ever heard
it felt good to help

Nan paid five times for the same gag
she said you were so clever

as the guards watch
I move dry
hard potatoes
around my moulded plastic plate
the others at the table
share jokes that turn me cold
starched collar rubs my neck
I can smell piss and detergent
John looks at me
'it's your turn kid'
before I can tell him

I only know one
the buzzer goes

you are somewhere
laughing
with music and girls
staying up talking films and
being funny
you know more jokes now

Me:

It's Thursday
six a.m. and staying in bed's for grown ups
we've finished dreams of being the fifth member of the A-Team
stuff getting blown up
me and you
are sharing a bed
because we have to but
no need for a brave face
cos to us it's a racecar
    base or
a spaceship
so we're glad to and
every morning
I wake up
my face   next to your feet
and Nan wonders why I leave
for school
without anything to eat

two families under one roof
stupid queues for the bathroom but
to tell you the truth
we feel like the luckiest two ever
cousins   tighter than glue
play-fighting and writing the clues
to treasure hunts we never once
seem to see through
we tell people we are brothers
and construct complex booby traps
for our sisters using crude tools
and a few of Nan's new covers
  the others say that
I'm trouble
and that you're easily led
Steven puts stupid ideas in his head
and gullible Aaron agrees on the double

but right now
they're still sleeping
as we're creeping downstairs
the ingenious joke that I
                              I mean we
planned is gonna take some time to prepare
I fetch a knife
from the drawer in the kitchen
the one that we know we're not supposed to open
you stand guard nervously hoping
nobody's noticed
come on Aaron
you're hopeless but
I can't pull this off   on my own

and if it's gonna work like it should
then you've just gotta
do what you're told
now
fetch the ketchup
before she gets up and we get ketched
and have to stretch out hands to get whooped   come on

right
now you lie face down on the floor
1, 2, 3, 4 eight-year-old paces from the living room door
I wedge the knife
between your body and arm
say you've got to stay calm
just as we hear Nan's alarm
a quick splatter of red sauce   just for effect
pinch myself for fake tears
the whole scene is set
What's that?
You're not sure? What?
You think that it's mean?
I'm telling you this is gonna be the bestest joke ever seen, ever!

and then we hear her
the line between excitement and fear
becomes less clear as the footsteps on the landing
get nearer
here goes
now remember
pretend that you're dead
and before you can say anything

I'm into the hall bawling and
calling for help

I don't think I'll ever forget her face
or the pace at which her body flew
down those stairs
hairs on the back of my neck stand up and
it's strange how the greatest plans
have a knack of leaving you feeling completely
unprepared

I'd never seen Nan look scared
and the way she stared at me through tears
over your shoulder as she was holding you
told me
I'd broken something
        as you sat crying in each other's arms
I went cold and all I could hold was the
numbness

fast forward
a sixteen-year-old's boredom
other kids share sordid stories
truth or dare and
they always avoid the forfeit
   me?
   man
I've never even been kissed
opportunities missed because I felt scared of something

I see you less now
since you moved with your mom

she tells Granddad how the kids that you run with are wrong
Aaron's in with a bad crowd
he says
            and the days I sit with him
he talks of you
and how it'll all end in tears
this from a man with fewer friends than cold beers
and his old ears won't hear
the white noise of his own fears
cheers
he says
here's to the one who done good
off to college
then university
just like he should
why can't some of what you've got
rub off on your cousin?
I don't tell him we got high just last night
shared a dozen cans
of cheap booze even he wouldn't drink
            it's just easier to keep quiet
allow him to think
what he wants
            he's not able to see how he's trapped me
cos it's more important to appear stable
than ever feel happy

I don't mention it was you who told me
what kind of beer he likes or
how you stepped in and saved me
in so many fights
it's not even funny

but a big heart won't get far
with him
it won't buy you a house to live in
it's not money

Him:

My first time
they asked me why not
and I couldn't think of a reason
fine rain fell
and I didn't have my coat
the quick kiss of the needle and
feeling warm
touching my own smile as I sat
on the wall
outside Mom's house

I couldn't look her in the eye
so I went straight to bed and
purple dreams

him who can't hear must feel
Nan said
back then it justified
us getting the slipper
now it justifies conversations
about me and my mistakes
words to wash your hands of me

people always want to know why
        I guess
I just had less reason
not to
one step to calm comfort
and after a while my body needed it

I didn't want help
I just wanted
to sit at the same table as my family
him who can't hear must feel
I guess
there must be something wrong
with my ears

Me:

It's Thursday

the piece of paper
gun-stapled to the wall of this
supposed place of higher learning
says
        I'm ready to start earning
I somehow scraped a pass

part of me feels to laugh
but I don't
move
as my unknown classmates
go shouting past

Granddad said he wants me to talk
to you
now that you're out
but what the hell could I ever
try and teach you about
real life?

I'm coming home with ten grand
of debt
twelve stitches
a tattoo and the obligatory
idea for a book
but as far as anything remotely resembling
a plan for what now
I'm stuck

see I've got friends   who are teachers
and friends   who are drug dealers and
if truth be told at least half
of the drug dealers   are teachers
and when word reaches
that I'm back around they'll be ringing me soon
to catch up and go down
to the local
and the joke'll be me
broke with a degree
and it won't take long before one of those
supposed mates is proposing to me
an idea
which is clearly a bad one
but doesn't sound so mad
after I've had one too many beers

and been thinking about the years
it'll take me till all my debt's cleared

Right Stevey, here's what you do
apply for a graduate job
doesn't matter what
just join with the ranks
of the frustrated office mob and
as you listen to their daily moan
stay quiet
open an account
and get yourself a graduate loan

ten grand in your hand
bring it to me
and you'll see
just how easy
making money can be
I'll put the rest to get a key
          twenty-three thousand
                    in total
then believe me
we're ready

36 ounces in that kilo
and each one of those ounces
breaks down into seventy
0.4g parcels that we know
move at street level
for twenty quid each and
shit mate
you don't have to teach maths

to crunch those numbers
20 x 70 x 36
£50,400 just for kicks

taking our twenty-three grand
and some overheads
off it
that leaves us with £25,000 profit
ten for you
fifteen for me
and we're sweet
should take roughly a month with demand on the street
how it is   now it is   of course
completely up to you
I'm just stating the facts mate
what d'you wanna do?

        a vision of the near future
sat at a computer
using software I'm used to
doing absolutely nothing
that excites me and before
 reality bites me most likely
I'll have no hair and kids
I don't see
I'll resent younger me
for being what I know I won't be
or
       I take a risk now
and get my head above water
my debt gone

I'll sign on, get to work on that book
stay at Mom's
keep her happy
clean and cook and who knows
in a year
it just might get accepted and I'm off   a well-respected writer

right
that's it
I'm decided   first thing
get a shit job
and that loan
that's what I'll do

then just as I drop off
my mind falls on you

Him:

As I step onto the bus I feel
people watching
I tell myself to remember
they don't know me
three weeks clean
as I move down the aisle between strangers
wondering if any of them
have done what I've done
and   there you are

at the back
leant against the window

in late afternoon light
cheap grey suit
world on your shoulders

you don't see me sit down
staring out at our streets
but I can see
you don't have a clue what you're doing

I remember that look
in the mirror of a shop window
a young man
       with no one to talk to

I still see him sometimes
through rain and
the stares
of strangers

nights dark as the shelter
between buildings
and the cold sounds a town makes
when people go to their homes
I don't say a word
as you get up to do
what you think
you have to do   but

I still recognise
my own face

BROKEN

To those
of what they call
broken homes
X-rays show up close two broken
domes
sipping cans while they're smoking cones
but always show respect with well-spoken tones
family moans
        they know it's a tragedy
many a night a dem spent up in casualty
cos if it's a fight then you know
        he had to be
        backing the underdog happily
but young paws can't fight laws
of gravity
lay in the gutter feel the moment
of clarity

that's the vision
make a decision
hear the voice in the back of the mind
time to listen
stop
aftershock of the brain
a few twitches
in a room with umpteen new stitches
and yes
        the nurse was cute

but you're stupid
just another mug a thug she can't do with

and maybe just for a second   your eyes meet
but then she gets you
back on your feet
and out on the street
she may have seen that beneath
the foolish meat
is a boy who's warm
          cool and sweet

it doesn't matter
          battered and
          clattered
and as a matter of fact
you'll probably see her next week cos

underneath the warm glove lies a fist
ever-ready to throw when eyes are pissed
and there's no bull of a man
denies the mist
when the flames reach boiling point   the fire's kissed

and they say
          He's mad at himself
and they say
          He's crying for help
and they say
a whole lot of stuff
as they watch from afar what they don't
live themselves

maybe they're right
but when he gets in a fight
he's not thinking about mental health

eyes roll back
he's not sure where it comes from
he comes to
and he sees they've all done one
and he's there
swinging   at   air
tongue struck dumb young grizzly bear
          bloody lip
          tears on his face
he thinks about family
thinks of disgrace
then

he picks himself up
runs home at full pace
huddled in corner   drunk and blood taste
prays for sleep
deep like oceans to
dream of beautiful girls and love potions
it's all good
          it's all bad
it's all good
          it's all bad

IT'S ALL GOOD

young blood with heart of an ox
held back in the school of hard knocks

sometimes   I don't see him for months
a few new cuts
one or two new lumps
we hear the sirens sound   my man jumps
I avert my eyes from bloodstain
on new pumps

we pull pints of pain
and pure pleasure
good times you can't measure unfold
the mind's treasure
and
peace
beautiful release   unspoken
barriers all broken smiles   we're all joking
but
then someone flicks the switch
Yo, he said
that she said
somebody
called our mom a bitch

What?!

rage
          aimed at a phrase

makes
eyes red
job done
guy's dead   mob run

the aftermath
broken noses
friendships
hope and glass   Hulk smash
I sometimes wonder how long can it last?
The cycle hits me
when I see your son in your lap

I know you fight
          cos it's all a fight
and if you're warm at night
          then it's all alright
but
as long as you breathe you won't fall tonight
I guess
          it must run in the genes

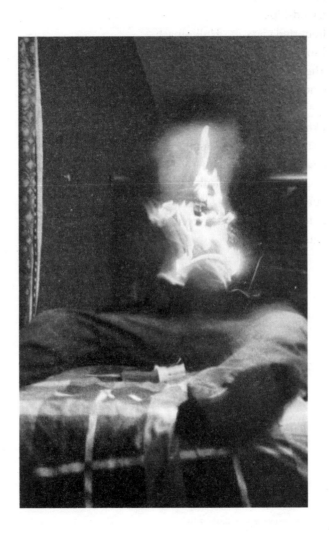

DANNY

Grey day
we're outside anyway
everything and nothing to say
stood by the wall
everything's boring when you don't have a ball
girls are the enemy
Danny's been telling me
he's older than me
and with that extra year
he's grown bolder than me
some kids think they're cool
but Danny's colder   you see

I stand with him almost every breaktime
and he takes time to tell me things
and when the bell rings
he just stands there
I don't care
he says
Them teachers don't know nothing
We did double negatives last week
but I keep bluffing
Nah, I know
I say
Who needs dumb sums and a village with three corners?
What you talking about?!
he says like a warning and
I make a mental note
to remember to stay quiet

our diet consists
of Wham Bars
Wotsits and Irn-Bru
Danny has a habit of lying
and I wanna be like him
so I'm trying too
So who would you choose?
he says and
I realise I'm not listening
        I was smelling the after-rain
and admiring
        the tarmac glistening
Are you listening? You baby! Come on,
start paying attention. Either your mom
or your dad has to die, who do you choose?
Answer the question!

a horrible thought
but I'm caught in the peer pressure
most days I'm hating the bell
now I'm praying that teacher appears
ding dong
so I seem to be saved by the bell
but the question's engraved like a spell on my mind
Danny just stands with his plans to play rebel

                          and I?

I walk hand in hand with the question
inside
either Mom or Dad has to die
ignoring the reasons why
I must choose
and before home time

I love my dad
he never checks my homework like Mom
or fusses about school
he's cool
he says I have to make my own rules
he rules!
I can see him deep thinking
while he's stood at the sink
he's not tight with his money
and turns real funny at night
when he's having a drink
he says one day he'll teach me to wink
but not right now
          cos I know that he's busy
some days he spins me round
          with his hand and
I have to sit down cos I'm dizzy

my dad is the boss

he's always working
he hides treasure he drinks
from a bottle that stinks
in the basket we keep dirty shirts in
nothing ever hurts him
          he's pretty much perfect
and if I close my eyes and try hard
I'm sure I can hear his voice
and though Mom cooks my food
and takes away
my bad moods
I'm sure Danny thinks that Dad's the right choice

I don't eat with the rest
cos I'm trying my best
to avoid what I know must be coming
my stomach feels tight
under my white cotton vest
it feels like my chest's got a drum in
some kids come running
from inside the hall and
I wish I was small or a hundred feet tall
so I could hide from Danny
or threaten to squash him
but I'm not
my face and my palms feel hot

      I don't like this game
I'm pretty sure I love Mom and Dad the same
and I know Danny hasn't got a mom
but I'm not to blame
we're just not the same
nah
he's better   cos he's older
and just then I feel a hand
on my shoulder
for a split second I think of my dad
then my mom
      then my dad again
and before I have a chance to feel sad again
his voice says
So who would it be? I didn't forget
I turn round to face him and must look upset
cos he says
Don't be such a girl! Just choose! It's easy!

and though I feel queasy
    I know
    what I'm supposed to say

Mom. My mom would die
and I'd live at home with my dad

it feels like a weight
has come off my shoulders
and now I've told him
it's not that bad
Danny smiles and I feel warm inside
as I think about all he's been telling me
he says
Moms are pretty much grown-up girls
and remember, girls are the enemy

a ball flies past and at last I've impressed him
passed the test and
    avoided a dare
so we start to play
and though the day's still grey
I have to say
I really don't care

DAVID

David was a kid I used to play with
in primary school
we'd end our days with
high fives
raise a Tip Top to future lives
choose our favourite members
of 5-Star for our future wives

we had sisters about the same age
both had family who came from overseas
demographic same page
same rage
in our heads from lack of role models
neither of us shut out
neither one mollycoddled
tight
taking turns for staying overnight
playing up late talking about
what the future might yield
him with the sword
me with the shield
spit on the palm
friendship was sealed

we hit eleven and split
moved house
new crowd
new school
same normal shit

next time I saw him
we were seventeen taking a hit
house party
cheap booze
and weed
the full bit
he told me about his brand-new Nova
with full kit
had a laugh
remember we could both do the full splits
weak moustaches on top lips
above broad smiles
lifting kiwi 20/20 full sip

he said he didn't do exams
obviously the weight of expectation
didn't fit into his plans
he'd rather do stuff with his hands
said he had plans to lay brick   squeeze tits   and sip
  cans

I told him I was off to college
to learn
he told me he was off to the car park
to burn
and just like that he was gone
the guy who helped me put my Batman suit on
rode off to where we were from

I blink and I'm twenty-one
back home
       fully grown

running and studying all done
life lessons mixed in with fun
that's all good and well but when it comes to the plans
I've got none

I've got the wallet of a nun
mind confused my body
                bruised my head spun
pub
couple of Guinness and cheap grub
out on the street I feel the base of a real sub-
woofer
guess who it is
he calls my name
he looks completely different   yet somehow
the same
we play the idle chit-chat game
then he tells me to get in
and pulls off – rubber and raw flame
Oh you're smart now? Can pick my simple mind apart now?
Lifting up the seat? Get out the bath to fart now?
I stay shut
and fight the lava gurgle in my gut
the truth is
                the pair of us are plainly in a rut
                two paths
                a few laughs
                equal shares of skids

he pulls out his wallet and shows me his two kids
Jesus Dave, you're a dad. Who's the mother?
One with the first girl, next with another

I'm feeling like a copper undercover
out of place but
somehow like this guy's my brother
and man it's not even a thing
whatever we've done since we both have wounds that still sting
I still keep my dad's ring
                          and David?
David still worries about what flowers to bring

Pop in the tape let's have a sing. Remember this old thing?
  STOP!
What?
Hammer Time!
                    we cruise around the old streets

first kiss
first spliff
shop where the pair of us stole sweets

I get to thinking these are the beats to people's lives
me still searching for something to feel alive
David just got out of 'the Green' on 3–5
and as I get out the car

I'm twenty-five

so you blink and you're twenty-five and
you've forgotten lots of things that made you feel alive
          open your eyes you're thirty-five
          with little lives
you now have to love
provide for

and guide
        turn around you're forty-five
and a woman who used to be an angel
is lying by your side

blink twice you're fifty-five   sixty-five
and it seems
things move too quickly   for your eyes
somebody said it's only
the foolish man tries to fight
the bright light that appears
through the grey of
                stormy skies
through all the secrets and lies
you start to realise
that finding yourself
is real wise

DEATH-PROOF

These lead shoes
you gave me when I met you
make sure I'd never forget you
it's funny what our heads do

we play games
you test me   I test you
some things hit
        others never get through
like how you'd ever think that I would let you

tell me what I do is to impress you
does your one have green eyes?
Guess Who?
you

yes you
the best I'm ever likely to get next to
the one who punched my chest through
and pressed mute
left me like a spider in a test tube

the devil in a red dress blessed you
with the gift that never left you
you never heard a word
I'd endeavour to suggest to

you
        you

the best I'm ever likely to get next to
the one who pulls my strings
      then lets loose
just when I'm sure that I get you

you tell me that together we could never be death-proof

it's like floating in the ocean in the rain
the fucked-up notion of holding onto pain
to sink solo
I keep a hole in my thoughts

think polo
halo
just a trick of the light
another kiss and I might   bite

you
and leave marks

freight train fights between us we leave

sparks

and keep scars on clean hearts

we build it up
we pull it down
I guess that's the fun of it somehow
I guess that's the trouble with sundown

the dark has to come out

FINGERS

Your mouth moves and
I notice little grooves above your lip
my mind slips and I'm a desert
a barren million miles
          a billion smiles of hollow glass teeth
beggar belief while
violent undercurrents pass beneath
irrigation
    no play   at this station
my feet rigid with concrete
a negative beat makes the pessimist
in me complete
as I eat bad news
drenched in white noise
girls and boys
let's have a warm hand
for young   bold   cold-souled soldier
toe to toe with the only older ever known
grown tenfold emotional   holder
so I told her
touch me
so when your eyes close
you don't lose me
choose me
so when the sun comes up
you won't use me

I'll get a whole troop of girl scouts to beatbox
and have 'em spittin' an unwritten rhythm

so fitting and deep the whole street rocks
and to this beat
I'll relay through wordplay
a new verse written with the warm air
you exhale   as you're sleeping
my pen weeping
leaving letter-shaped footprints
and even the ~~caged bird~~
~~is struck mute by your beauty~~
the sweet fruit that suits me   like passion
holding like it's going out of fashion
imagine
we know more about the moon's surface than the seabed
and sixteen times more about the seabed
        than I ever could about this feeling
my body reeling

and if I were able
I'd make my navel a portal
to release this gut feeling through a cable
straight to yours
                    pause
shared cause
        fingers intertwined

we'll open doors

CREATURES OF HABIT

It starts normal

the four of us in the car
        usual formation

Alex driving
Sean behind him
next to Adam in the back and
me
passenger seat

it's not like it has to be like that
we just never seem to change places

creatures of habit
driving between the same places
on a hazy day-by-day basis
praying the last week of summer takes   ages

like it used to

see we got used to our roads
those grey open gateways
between our homes
and the places we always go
we own them

self-crowned
soon-to-be-eighteen-year-old

Kings of Birmingham   well
our part at least
          car parks policed by old men
fighting retirement
providing the desired hiding spots
while we skin up and discuss pin-ups
see
Sean and Alex are always more
Pamela Anderson
while me and Adam have designs
on Liv Tyler
the focus of our desires should give you an idea of the kind
of time I'm talking about

this particular time
as we're driving and talking it out
we're making our way to the big Tesco
to buy booze and portable barbeques
for a little soirée in the park
before a party we're going to later
over in Selly Oak where the uni kids live

it's Saturday afternoon and
none of us
have a clue about what's coming

Alex can get served
seeing as
he's had nearly a full beard since
the second or third year
          the crunch of third gear punctuates
our conversation

a full stop at the end of his statement.
              Yo, Sarah looked a bit like Liv Tyler
   he keeps his eyes on the road
as he's driving while the six eyes
behind and beside him widen
in a confused silence
broken
by a response composed
of three voices speaking at once –
              What?
Alex, now aware of us staring
juggles our puzzled looks
while pulling into the turn-off
for the Tesco car park
              She did. I mean she had that look

time out

Alex is the only one of us with wheels
I can't even drive legally and
neither can Adam
                        Sean can but
he's got more chance
of bagging Pamela Anderson
than us letting him drive   see
Sean's got what we call
a slight   disregard for life
  he doesn't want to die but
         to the outside eye
he sometimes seems like he's trying

like the time
he tried to jump between
          the two highest trees
in the woods
arms and legs spread out from the middle
T-shirt stretched out
like a flying squirrel
          for a second it was beautiful
          the three of us gazing at grace in motion

next second he lay at our feet
wrist and ankle broken and when Alex
asked who to phone Sean just said
          No one

back to Alex and   his car
a whole summer spent stacking shelves
at the aforementioned Tesco spending
less dough led to
a sky-blue Fiesta
B reg
          last Alphabet

the first time he pulled up
outside college we didn't even
acknowledge him
cos it wasn't obvious it wasn't
one of the lecturers
trying to get on with us

the horn sounded
like when you die on *Super Mario* but

none of us laughed and
as a couple of rich kids walked past
and sniggered
all three of us cut them
a look to let them know if they wanted
a kicking
we'd happily give it

they didn't

our sky-blue carriage to freedom
now it's for that reason
the dynamic between us
is sometimes uneven see
we don't just love Alex
like a brother
we need him
so now
even though
I completely disagree
with his statement about Sarah
a girl he had a two-week thing
with over Christmas and New Year's
I proceed with appeasement

Yeah. She was pretty

I feel the carbon dioxide level
inside the car increasing
with Sean's audible sighs
from the back seat
and in the tiny mirror

in the fold-down sun guard
I see him over my shoulder
shaking his shaved head and
rolling his eyes

inside
　　　　the white of the aisles
　　　　is blinding

we divide to speed
up the finding

　　　　No White Lightning!
Alex warns
as me and Adam walk
towards the booze leaving Sean
and him to argue over barbeques

the two of us move
　　　　through partial families and staff like
　　　　Tron bikes and at one point
as we crisscross between
a young mom and her tearful son
　　　　we double high-five like Maverick and Goose
in *Top Gun* without breaking stride
and as we move back into formation
our mouths synchronise
smiles wider than our eyebrows

Adam's lanky
　　　　we call him Earthworm Jim cos

from certain angles it looks
a bit like he's got no chin

me and him love films   the summer before senior school
we worked our way through
every video at the corner shop
until we'd seen them all
and I knew that if I quoted
Escape from New York
when I was just talking
Adam would be the only one who'd know
    I don't want lager
he says as we stand
in front of a wall
of booze trying to choose
    Me either. But we can't get cider after last time
I'm not carrying Sean anywhere tonight
    Agreed. Rum, then

two bottles of Havana Club
three of ginger beer
and one pack of plastic cups and
we're done

meeting the other two
we hand Alex the booty
and step back to admire
his underage skill from the safety
of the magazines
    if not for him
we'd have just been four
seventeen-year-olds walking the streets

dreaming of being older
   the joke is
   he's only
two months older than me   but
if I wore shorts and a vest
and he dressed in slacks and a flat cap
he could probably pass for my dad

the three of us watch in awe
as he gives a masterclass in small talk
staying blasé as he pays   at one point even making
the middle-aged till lady blush and look away
and I'm just about to sing his praises
when Sean cuts in –
         Sarah looked like Liv Tyler? I don't remember Liv Tyler
         having a bum chin
                  Bum chin?
Adam questions
Sean cups miniature
imaginary buttocks
underneath his mouth
me and Adam laugh out loud
         What's funny?
Alex asks as the four of us
walk through the automated doors
Sean's eyes smile widely
         Just telling these two about John Travolta.

hindsight is a bully

   we cruise along the dual carriageway
in our sky-blue jewel

as the blood-orange sun
slides over the horizon
  Sean's homemade TDK
in the tape deck plays *36 Chambers*
with warped bass
and for what feels like ages
no one says a thing
as we all just enjoy
  the freedom
  of moving to a soundtrack

I can see us   I remember the feeling

four young men getting ready
for whatever the world outside
our young Brummie bubble held we felt
  together and separate
at the same time
then
  as we turn
into the woods
as if by telepathic agreement
we all join in on exactly the same rhyme
  Hey, you, get off my cloud
  You don't know me and you don't know my style...

some things are perfect
  just for as long as it takes
  to say the words in your head and
even now
knowing the very fucked-up worst
  of what

happened
just a few hours later
that's the feeling

I try not to forget

FRONT STEP

A sky full of endings
each star a full stop
still   he aims high
mind stubborn as a bulldog
jumper gets pulled off
and given to another
fifteen whole minutes
after meeting one another
cover me   I'm going in
he thinks
blood mixed thin with
adrenaline and drinks   just ask
bask in the warmth
of your wishes
can a thought
be sought
in the talk
before kissing
an unknown stranger
sitting on the front step
of full-blown danger
young lone ranger
looking for a lover not a sidekick
somebody to ride   into a life with
somebody to find a little time with
caught in between dreams
and the means of surviving
deep breath

look into her iris
does it feel like her insides
want me to dive in?
I'm not even like this
he thinks
blood mixed thick with
adrenaline and drinks   just timing
her lips move slow
like a flower opens
Why you smiling?

and just like that   his legs fail
and just like that   she gets mail
just like that they exhale
their future opens
      ship sets sail

listen

children sleeping
  a young man and woman
sip wine in the kitchen   quietly speaking
food on plates but
he's not eating
something in the air
like a gas pipe leaking
tell her what you're feeling   he thinks
blood mixed thin
with adrenaline and drinks   just say
pray she's feeling the same
life as a family
the crazy game that we're playing

staying in   no sleep
dreams are decaying
steadily resenting the roots that we're laying
straying from a handed-down path   well-worn
instead of a regret for a net well torn
I miss us
and rather than battle with mistrust
I think we should discuss
deep breath
       look into her iris
       does it feel like her insides
       are crying for what mine is?
I'm not even like this
he thinks
blood mixed thick with
adrenaline and drinks   just timing
her lips move slow
like a flower opens
why don't you try smiling?

and just like that   his legs fail
and just like that   he turns pale
just like that they exhale
their future broken
       foes set sail

listen

street light leaks through
       wallpaper desert
       an old man sits focused
measured

stares at the pattern blindly hoping
for treasure
pouring another dark rum from the dresser
lesser men than me live happily   he thinks
blood mixed thin with
adrenaline and drinks   relax
bask in the warmth
of your wishes
a thought sought before the force of the vicious
from a man left empty
          sitting in an armchair
          surrounded by plenty
          knife cuts gently when you hold it

in your own hand
no more colour when the whole palette
goes bland
looking at the picture of a grown man   looking back
          a vision of the spring through the eyes of a snow man
deep breath
          look into the iris
          does it feel like my insides
          are crying for the violence?

I'm not even like this   he thinks
blood mixed with
paracetamol and drinks   it's all timing
his hand moves slow
like a flower opens
why you smiling?

and just like that   his legs fail
and just like that   he looks frail
just like that   he exhales
his future closes
          soul sets sail

listen
can you hear the
listen
train of a life getting nearer
listen
might be yours
listen
best mind the closing doors
could it be any clearer?

listen

INSIDE

Day breaks
at a pace that makes the face ache
and   just for his faith's sake
he tries to stay calm
   looks down
at his young man's hands and arms
and remembers a time
they seemed so much smaller

      outside it's grey
and as the rain beats a rhythm
on the windowpane
inside feels just the same
      he remembers the game
      he used to play
      home alone
racing the raindrops
to the edge of the glass

back then   he only had to ask
any questions
there was always someone inside
who seemed to have the answers

in that house that smelled
of fresh pumpkin
fried dumplin'
beans and Saturday cartoons

old tunes   Lee Perry and James Brown
when Soul II Soul came round
he was rocking a fade
Super Mario got played
and played
like the hand-me-down jungle tapes
        his brother gave him from raves

everything was simple and nice
Granddad's advice
Nanna cooking peas and rice for ten children
cousins did the running man
and whether it was sunny out and hot   or not
it never really mattered

        first time he ever got battered by four kids
or on four quid's worth of Tennent's Super
shared with James Cooper
both times he got the same feeling
that all he wanted to be
was back inside home

inside
nothing could hurt him   the fortress

Castle Greyskull
with Mom as the Sorceress
of course
things changed
people died   people left
people lied   some turned strange

outside became home
two steps from fully grown
running with a crew but
in truth   all alone

sitting in the park
hitting spliffs and getting high
not really fitting in   not really knowing why
different
only thing in common was boredom
keeping score of how many lips and trips they'd had
it went bad   the same old role play
picking up the dole pay and
smoking
to find home

          inside and outside got blurred
so when he got hurt the only places to go
were the dark rooms
and now he's sitting in
going out less and less
smoking sess   got in a mess
internal voices
          blames himself for bad choices
and with only himself to convince
it's a cinch to hear voices

no outside
inside became both
one minute a haven
next second a nightmare
the whole world   is right there

one third of an inch
of that same glass
is now too much
to ask

it's grey
on both sides
and nothing tastes worse
in this world   than wasted time

at this point the narrator steps up
out of the paper and slaps his face
to wake himself
it's now ten years later

days rolled by
an avalanche of years
tears run off flushed cheeks
and drown in his beers

it appears that things change
and people move on
but if you just squint your eyes
that perception is wrong
inside to outside
                it's nobody's choice

but what better way
of getting out
than using my voice

JESSICA

Fifteen and
       I'm sparking a joint
in the park with the boys
chatting fart   making noise
the girls are on a bench
over there in the distance
to put space between
our best means of resistance

it's getting dark
and we all wanna kiss them
but we don't have a clue
what to do so we just
diss them
          too embarrassed
to talk it over
then John's like,

Hold on, somebody's walking over
Oh no yo, it's two of the girls

the other half of the species
confusing our world
if they choose you
it proves you're mature to the world
    fingers crossed in my pocket
    foot's moving the dirt

never sure whether   they're gonna smile or bite you
they walk right over
like they're ready to fight you
they both look at me and say
Jessica likes you
my mind goes numb
my mouth's like   *alright cool*

let me tell you 'bout Jessica Brown
every single maths lesson
          I've been checking her out
something in her eyes
makes my chest wanna shout and
that freckle
by the neck of her blouse
I'm like   wow

turns out
she'd been checking me too
and though I never asked her out
she'd been expecting
me to
so   just for good measure
extra pressure to boot
now my penalty's up but
am I ready to shoot?

at this point
I know I'm supposed
to follow 'em
and if anyone's got kissing techniques
I wanna borrow 'em

I can't swallow
and the possible horror of tomorrow
if I get it wrong's
got me hollow
I can't breathe
   it'll be worse if I run so I can't leave
and I've got no control
over the bones in my knees

my friends are egging me on
telling me
You can't leg it
if you leave now you'll regret it
believe

next thing I know
we're in the middle of the park
her friends   my friends watch

from afar

neither of us
even sure
where to start
the stars are coming out
the whole park's   getting dark

she looks at me
my mind goes numb
I try to fight the urge
to just pull her hair   and run

next thing I know
her tongue's touching
my tongue
and I'm not sure
if I'm doing it right but
I'm like
     nice one

for some reason I'm closing my eyes
the
whole
    park
      melts
        and
        we're frozen in time
her hand's on my shoulder
I'm holding
    her side
    then my hand goes down
    slowly strokes her behind
I don't know why
what a joker am I?
oh no says my mind   *something's poking her thigh!*
it's not how it's supposed
to unfold I won't lie
but she's holding me tight
just to show me
it's fine

this girl is wicked
and I wish we could kiss   forever

I hear my name and I try
not to listen
open my eyes   I'm in the foetal position

on my bed
aged ten
not even dreaming of kissing
        even getting into my clothes feels
like a mission
but I smell fried dumplin' from down in the kitchen
no television   in my room like I'm wishing
but there's football to play
to the park's my decision
Mom shouts up *I hope you've got your vest on!*
and
even though I know that I don't I'm like *Yes, Mom!*
I know now
        it's better never to test Mom
forget TV detectives
        believe she's the best one

Can't stop, Mom, kick off's at two
Boy, come back after seven you'll catch a lick off my shoe

I smile as I leave
Raleigh Burn up the street
two dumplin' I'm eating too quickly
to chew

Welcome back to this forty-a-side
week-long grudge match
the score is 34-all

Steve gets the ball, out on the right
cuts back inside, square ball to John
John goes to turn, the crowd shouts MAN ON!
pass back to Steve, who lets loose a shot
you won't believe top right-hand corner
out of goalkeeper's reach
the team goes mad
PILE ON! Behind the goal' – man what's the time?

                          twenty to nine?
                          I'm like

                  oh

racking my brain
for an excuse
even though it's no use
I still choose to make one
Mom'll take none
but I've gotta   say something
close the front door
can still smell the dumplin'

I can't see Mom
so I dump my stuff
just enough time
to make tea and   butter her up

what time do you call this?

I don't reply   just act surprised
and close my eyes
to get licked

87

but
      the licks don't come
I stand struck dumb
      count down from five to one
then   I slowly open my eyes
to my surprise
I stand dressed smart   I'm now twenty-one

well done son   Mom gives me a hug
young man grown up, graduated and done

she wears her best clothes
and I don't suppose she knows
her son owes The Man ten grand
                  for fun

but right now
it don't matter
as she's sat chatting with Jess's mom and dad
over a cold platter
      they're all laughing how we're still together
from the side we watch them
drink wine
getting leathered
she looks amazing
better than I ever remember
in those lessons when she drove me crazy
she looks at me   a little nod for maybe
it's time we should tell 'em
      we're having a baby

open my eyes
I'm twenty-nine and
our eight-year-old son wants
to learn
how to rhyme
standing at the foot of our bed
and off the top
of his head
he spits a flow   showing perfect time

you know that deserves a smile

OK
let's get dressed
brush your teeth and we'll work on style
Get your clothes on
and don't forget your vest, lad
and even though I know that he won't he's like
      Yes, Dad!

a cup of tea in my mug
that says Best Dad
more rhymers in the house?
That'll be driving Jess mad
but she just smiles
as she sips her tea and as   I tickle her feet
he comes back
with his best pad

right
first thing
you must observe the time

a good flow is like a fossil
it preserves the time and
the only thing of worth you can learn from mine
is that the spaces between words deserve to shine
          you've gotta find your own style, son
and if the flow feels right to you the rhyme's done

sometimes looking back in time is good
cos some things don't change
as you find what you love
speak what you know
breathe deep as you flow
some people are gonna bite you
to keep the light down
and they can say what they like
but   when you're gripping a mic
just make sure that you rhyme
for right now

COMPTON

Once upon a time
in a land where
the men
tattoo LOVE & HATE both
on one hand
there lived a family

the average fabric
of a woman and a man
a girl and a boy
a few toys
and a cat   (her name was Whiskas)

most days they all sat happy
together but
some days
          plates smashed   against the wall
when they got flung
like
a discus

after a fight
the dad would play Black Sabbath
into the night
the mom would blast Eurythmics
in the kitchen
the kids would sit listening to both

the girl drawing the sky
the boy writing
his Christmas gift wish-list
in the form of a rhyme:

Dear Santa,
A calculator watch is what I want
and if you don't get me that
then you're a . . . really bad Santa

the girl
was an avid dirty dancer
watching Patrick Swayze
seven times a day
   till the VHS tape wore away
but
the boy wasn't into that
  his older cousins   already into rap
gave him a tape of N.W.A. and said

Listen, tell us what you think of that

so he went to his room
and put it on
then turned it off again.
Are you mad?
If Mom hears that
I'ma catch a slap
and I don't even
wanna think about Dad!

so he put it in an old sock
in a shoebox
       on top of his wardrobe
       underneath a blanket
       and told himself

       to forget it

he spent his afternoons
wrestling his little sister
       he was three years older
so it was easy to lift her
onto his shoulder
for an
       inverted
       tombstone

  she pretty much
did what he told her
and liked it when he rolled her
up in her own duvet
like a sausage
in   *My Little Pony* pastry

They've been fighting a lot, lately

she said one afternoon
as he had her in the early stages
of a perfect
       Boston Crab

the boy knew   straight away
that this was one
of those
serious moments
in the middle of a game
that they every so often
had

he told her not to worry
        then finished her off with
        a suplex

Who's the greatest?
You are
Say it louder!
You are!
That's correct

later on
the girl sat   on the kitchen floor
playing the mom
at *Connect 4*
something felt wrong
she'd been keeping   score
but the mom hadn't won one
now the girl didn't miss a lot
but she failed
to spot
the fact Dad's coat   was missing
from the hook
on the back of   the door

Where's Steven?
        He's over there.
Doing his homework?
        No. He's watching that documentary
        about the frozen home of the polar bear

Again? Well tell him his dinner's ready
I've made his favourite
turkey drummers and Alphabetti Spaghetti
but not in front of the telly
tell him to come to the table
I need to speak to you both
it's important

later that night
the boy sat alone   on his bed
one hundred and one
Carl Lewis-shaped thoughts
running
        through
                his head

Mom had said it wasn't their fault
it was just that Dad
        was confused

his sister had asked who they'd live with
and whether they'd have
to choose
and as she and the mom sat downstairs
on the sofa
in a state

the boy's eyes were drawn up
to the top of his wardrobe

his face changed and
a
cartoon lightbulb
appeared

      (and for those who don't know   this represents
   an idea)

downstairs
the living room was cold
curtains were closed and
the sofa
looked like an   old boat

in the middle of the ocean
both of them adrift
in it

he told them to stand up
handed them sunglasses
he got free with Happy Meals

they didn't ask him why
but as he moved past them
to the old Hitachi stereo
he looked back
and   his mom and sister
kinda looked like
the Blues Brothers

he pressed rewind on the tape
put sunglasses on his face
pressed play
          stood back
          and waited

as the music started
his mom and sister looked startled
so
he quickly explained the role play
and told them

You've just gotta trust me

Mom, you're Dr Dre. Sis   you're Eazy-E
Whiskas the cat can be MC Ren
and me
          I'm Ice Cube

for the rest of the night
they passed a wooden spoon like a mic
rhyming along
to all the tracks
          swearing as loud as they liked –

So when I'm in your neighbourhood, you better duck!
Cos Ice Cube is as crazy as fuck!
As I leave believe I'm stompin'
But when I come back, boy, I'm comin' straight outta Compton!

That's it, Mom, Compton!

and that's the tale of how N.W.A.
took a day that was gonna be grey
and just for a while at least
made it OK

And since that day
whatever mess I'm getting in
to feel better   I just

press play

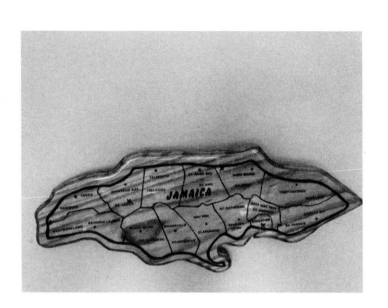

MOVES

Mobile phone   interferes with the speakers
two modern-day defeatist
creatures
sit resting

four a.m. and
all they've got is stones   in their bellies
three years between them but
      both have seen plenty
      jokes have been many
      International Superstar Soccer wonder goal highlights
      are silently looping on the telly

the pips echo
pre-empting a text message
they look at each other and
                  wonder whose phone's gonna get it

the older one frowns and downs
his now-cold brew
Ain't no news at four in the morning gonna be good
at that exact moment
the younger man's phone
goes into vibrate mode and
dances over the edge   of the broken coffee table

his face changes
as he breathes in
believing the phone screen's about to ruin his evening –

Yo, I think I'll just leave it. Give it a miss. Pretend I didn't hear it.
Ignorance is bliss. Yo play back the track again
I wanna hear what we recorded

the older man shakes his heads and points
No, it could be important

he picks up the phone and throws it over and
in one move
        his friend catches the phone
        and clicks the message open

both of them freeze
the evening's been productive
two tunes constructed   a few new rhymes been busted
now the atmosphere has been
severely interrupted
Man, will you just fuckin' read it?

the younger man smiles and
                        all tension is broken
the older man says
you're evil
and he's only half joking
Who's it from, that girl with the eyes?

Why's it always your phone that gets a lovely surprise?

Nah, mate, it's not a girl, it's from Davey
he says he was driving home and some DJ geezer
played me on the radio, he says it was crazy

people texting in saying they rate me   *apparently*
I'm making moves

the older man smiles then   without even blinking says
You reset the game mate
I'll get the drinks in

I just need to piss

Well hurry up
I'm ready to administer another arse-whipping
four-nil twice on the bounce mate   *you must be slippin'*

in the minutes it takes
for the tea to be made
the younger man reloads the game
and thinks about how strange it is
that strangers in faraway places now   know his name
Weird

What's weird?

the older man brings in the tea
                Arsenal vs Barça in large
                on the screen

It's weird that people actually heard me, you know what I mean?

Yeah, it's pretty crazy. You want a custard cream?

the game begins
a rundown of both teams

two faces glow in the light
from the screen
                they look young in this scene and in real terms
                they really are young in this
                scene of music

I dunno. I never really thought about it going any further
than us getting stuff recorded
don't you think it's a strange one?

the older one's voice changes tone
as though
        saying so
        after ages
        singing the same song
Look, lad. It's par for the course now, we're making moves
now shut up and focus
it's game on

            Word spreading that we might be alright
            invited to meetings to say what we think
            rich decision-makers with no ideas
            apparently we're making moves

                    you can't teach a new trick to old dogs
                but you don't got to if the old tricks are still sick
                          so roll on

            man I'm not worried
            about opinion
            I'm worried about
            the middle-men

who wanna put you in a hole
you couldn't even fit a pigeon in

I thought I saw my dad
he looked just like me
if I'd never figured out
what I wanted to be

apparently we're making moves

to anyone who thought we wouldn't do it
anyone who sat waiting for us to flop
so they could say
I told you
I knew it
they had their chance and they blew it
now they're just two dudes
who spend their afternoons in Wetherspoon's
hogging the pool
bumming a light
looking to fight   pretending at cool
cos it's not hard to be Fonzie
when you're
surrounded by Potsies

sitting in the hot seat
their specialist topic
is 'How They Got It and Lost It
then became Alcoholics'

supposedly sicker than vomit
but now you're old enough
to rock a bus pass inside your wallet
Oops

Reality check   that's us mate
and yeah we're still catching the bus
dust in our pockets trust me
we've got PhDs and our theses
are titled

'How to Make Three Pound Forty-Eight Pence Last a Week'

apparently

we're making moves

r e p e a T

And
   I ain't never been eloquent
all I've ever been into
         is trying to write real
             life down
that my friends will find relevant
so when I walk into a pub
and see ten of 'em
       and the
tension's heavy as an elephant
cos I ain't been back in time and
lack relevance
they think   I think they harbour raw jealousies
cos I seem like
I'm some kind of celebrity
seen on internet rhyming
about those times in the park
our best memories
          dark
stories we all know
now my best messages
atmosphere's barren as a desert is
with these men who went
and did heavy shit
hard selling it
suspended sentences
families
tired eyes
hard lives

delicate subject
     just get a drink
     and don't mention it
get a round in   commence with the pleasantries
old-time beef
     man deaded it and yet
     I still feel the sediment
settled in the bellies
of boys grown
never known more than their own back yard
the cold precipice
     slip into my old skin years after shedding it
old friends telling me
it's better that I left
they knew I had to get somewhere else
to reap benefits
     Deano leans in and tells me
     Jessica's the best thing he's ever seen and
     do I want a little bit of ketamine?

his eyes smile wide full of pessimist
Chelsea-brick elegance
and I really don't
     but then again
I know what a gesture is
and this is close as I'll get
to a welcome home benefit
he sits back and we laugh like old friends again
yes we're pretending
     but we're on the same level
and we both chose together – regression's the best medicine

regression's the best medicine

sometimes

I could never be
anything other than
me
since I was given
the *working men* element
      sentiment cold
      bold shoulders unfold into wings to sing relevance
I will not forget where I'm from
the strong genesis
trying to be the *Best of the Best* just like Eric is
      inside
      my own mind   no dependency
                      on anyone's opinion
                      no matter what their industry level is

you see me
      I crave better shit

something to find without being spoon-fed it
      I just want something to find without
      being spoon-fed it

so is there anybody out there?
if I throw out a line now   will anybody hear it?

is there anybody out there?
I was told there's some light   I'm just trying to get near it

is there anybody out there?
how come I feel alone in a room full of people?

is there anybody out there?
my heart is a scale

and I can't make it equal

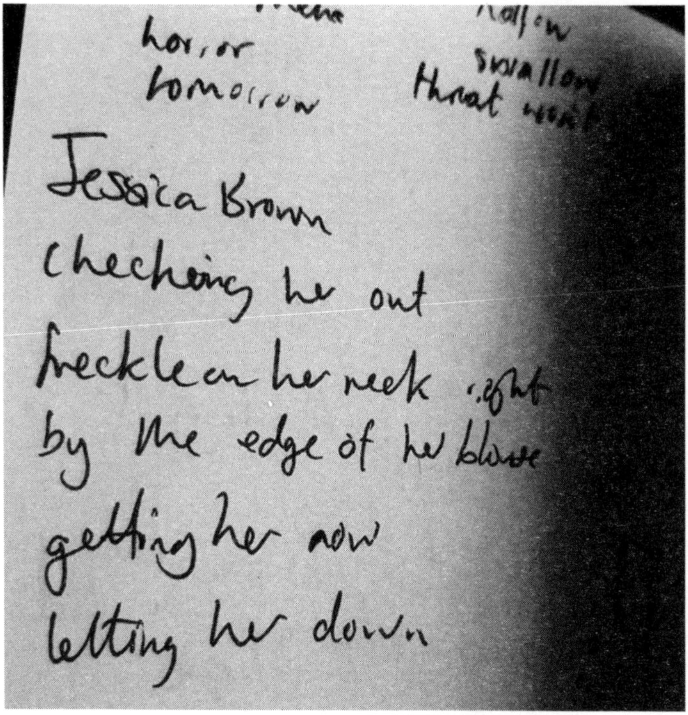
horror
tomorrow

swallow
throat

Jessica Brown
checking her out
freckle on her neck right
by the edge of her blouse
getting her now
letting her down

SCENE

for David J

Eyes open
feeling not too tough
I guess I still don't know when
I've had enough
     some things don't change

my old skull feels too small
for my young brain
and the old *no pain, no gain*
doesn't really apply
     to this one

spliff on
get a tea
have I got milk?
better see
     the habitual routine
     of a boy-man
     living his days

I blew 150 last night
now I'm digging for change
prince to pauper cliché
stuck on a loop

either I've got dough and I blow it
or I don't and I fucking know

it must be the price you pay
for living in the moment
you learn hard
     when old friends
are taking turns
to buy their own yards
it kinda leaves you looking at your own cards
     but
I coughed this morning and
some words came out of my mouth
reminded me what it is
that makes my world turn so
anyone who writes or plays

          for nights
          and days and fights to pay
          rent might relate
          to the position

of a visionary wishing
he'd be given   a wage

     to exist as well as scribble on pages

the stage is set
to make something
     out of nothing   like the A-Team
and I guess that's why
I never really sleep
         I daydream

see I used to run with John
back when Big Bird was

yellow
    I was Raphael
he was Donatello

together we moved up
to the big school
our Walkmans feeding us jungle and
        every male friend of the family
        seemed to be
        an uncle

we chased the same girls
tamed the same curls
had our first shaves
in the same sink
back at my mom's

John would stay at ours
        I'd stay at John's
we'd make beats
on the PlayStation
for our MC alter egos to speak on

Yo check it! This is the Polarbear,
and I'm live!
        I don't want four fish fingers
with my beans and chips
I want FIVE!

the clarity of mentality shared
all we cared about was dreams and
what we could do

last time I saw John
that could had become should and
he had three haircuts   ripped jeans and overly clean shoes

we went out
tipped a couple of rums
just an educated couple of bums
sat in a bar
me with no money   him with a fast car
him on a nine-to-five   me living to write
and
as I walked home that night
I thought hard
about how I had a new name
for my long list of safe
but different
mates

see   people move
        in nuff different ways
        at different rates
        and all I could think was   broke or not

I really can't complain

  I
  think

the grass is always greener
but I'm happy
with my own grass

all I'm after is a little bit of green
to buy my own gas
starting up my own class:
Polarbear's 'How to Be Not Shit in 3 Simple Steps'
man don't laugh

Step 1: Become extremely good at something
Step 2: Keep on getting better and
Step 3 if you're wondering is a warning

if you're ever completely happy
with what you've done
you'll go to sleep thinking you're good
and wake up shit in the morning   I promise

lesson over
Mr Polar,
go to the front of the class
and show these
so-called pros
how they're supposed to do it

you know something's good
when it seems
you already knew it
man   stop talking about that idea and do it
Get Shit Done mate

imagine writing something
that reaches people
on a level and equal   leaves them needing a sequel
getting right to the point like

the brown in the needle of the guy you   stepped
    over in the street
on your way to the latest night
full of the 'right people'

see there's a reason they call it a 'scene'
        it's cos it's not real
it's just a role play
same characters   different hairstyles

what used to get him vexed is now making a bear smile   man
whatever blows your hair back   just gimme my free drink

if I was here for the money   I'd be rich by now
if I listened to all the talk   I'd be a bitch by now
and when I say bitch
        I don't mean a derogatory term for girls
        I refer to the worms
        only concerned   with what they hope   is cool

cos people   let's face it
if lyrical ability and brilliant delivery
    made you famous
    every single one of us would be wearing   David J trainers

so why say in ten lines   what you can say in just two
and why say in two lines

what you can shut up and do

SCOTCH

All of this
is for four years
spent doing one-man
bedroom concerts for my cat

can I get a miaow at the back?

can I get a miaow at the back?   she never answers back

picture a boy   stood in front of a mirror
he's about 24% shorter than me
54% more awkward
and about 14% thinner
he's holding an old afro comb
to his lips   shifting his weight
                between his feet   every piece
                of his persona fits a beginner

he dreams of being a winner
and in this picture
winning means being part of world-champion
battle-rap tag teams   so
as a long-haired ginger cat
cleans her own privates
three feet away
   on the windowsill
   our young hairbrush MC
       psyches himself up to start rhyming

freeze him

in the breath before speaking
lungs full   we leave him and cut
to the kitchen downstairs
where an older boy with
a shaved head stares at his hands as a kettle
comes to the boil

he's wrapping small blocks
                  of something
                  into mini tinfoil packages
as he stands all
Air Max
pin-rolled jeans and NAF NAF

we hear a man's laugh
through the wall
and for a second the older boy doesn't
move at all

then he carries on   only quicker
twisting the last little brick
between thumb and index finger
he swings a rucksack off his shoulder
                  and opens it
                  slipping the bricks in
                  the look on his face
a mix of excited faith
                        guilt   and grin

freeze him

in the breath before wiping the sideboard
clean
we leave him and cut back
to upstairs where the long-haired
ginger cat just stares
back at our young rhymer
        as he wraps up his verse
        something like

Yeah, cos you know
if flows were clothes
then the bear would wear a monocle
oracle lines leave weak minds
full of dread
like Rastafarian hair follicle, oh!

nothing

no applause
cos even if she could
clap with her paws
she probably wouldn't
                see
she's seen him work
on his battle face
so any cat he'll face will
be smashed away   but
        that's not to say 'cat'
        as in slang for fellow artist

that's actual cats   like feline
cos the only ears
he's rhymed to
are those of the cat
he's currently stroking
who pretty much shows love
                    regardless

she's watched him work
on his best faces and
gesticulations
watched him rhyme half naked
post-shower
boasting about his flow power and seen him
come home low
          after bottling it hard at parties
so instead   she just coughs
               drops off the windowsill
               rubs herself against his leg as she passes him
               down the stairs
                    slipping out through the front door
                         just as the older boy pulls it closed

we hear him call back   *Yo, I'm back late!*

     then watch him bounce
up the short pathway to where another
young man waits against the wall
Ready?
Yeah
                    the dovetail of knuckles
as the pair of them look up

towards the open bedroom window
hearing 'The World Is Yours'
come pouring out into the air

Yo, your brother still rhyming?
All the time man. To himself

freeze them

in the breath between
a good choice
and a really   really bad one
we leave them

I hear people
say *fortune favours the brave*
but
what if fortune
is just the simple bliss
of the risk that you take?
    so one day's grace
    is another's mistake and
    being forced to wait
  might be the force that saves
they tell me
You've gotta get with the times, right?
How else you gonna get
a bit of time in the limelight?
            but
I'm like
            limelight?
            who signed up for that?

I guess I must've done
just to come to a place
where the race
to be great's just begun
stuff I used to do just for fun
has become   what puts food
on the table

so am I able to make it?
              facing my chance   am I able
                      to take it down
look round at the mates
I was raised with
chained
to the places they feel safest

              I don't think I'm better than them
              I just will not settle with them
feels like there's something
I'm after
so many paths I just have to
choose

could've been a dealer   could've been a teacher
didn't wanna be that *should've been* geezer
preaching to people he could've been a hero
I'm telling ya, I could've made it
but nobody cares
        except him
life was a morning and man slept in
bitterness came and the rage
crept in

and now it's eating him inside out
till the ringside towel gets   thrown in
and the man in the mirror
is his only opponent
and if you're thinking   how do I know this?

it's because I know him

he comes each night
when I'm dreaming
I wake up scared   mouth silently screaming

                    I can see him
                    can't be him
                    the sign on my heart says *carpe* . . .

so this
          is for four years
          spent doing one-man
          bedroom concerts for my cat

can I get a miaow at the back?

can I get a miaow at the back?

SEVEN-THIRTY

Seven-thirty and
I'm knackered again
but you know I'm up and at it again
that's how it's gotta be
I have to tell myself   it's not a lottery
just put in the time and
the rest will work properly
   I've gotta be wary of the clock
and how it's stopping me
cos resting on the stock that I've got
that's a false economy
work on my stance for the chance
somebody's knocking me
                  but
word on the street
is the bear is hot property
   I click the kettle on
tapping the cup with my spoon
tapping along with my feet and
pretty soon
I can feel I'm building a beat
that's how it goes
where it comes from   who knows?

and I don't suppose it matters
whether or not I chose to live by a rhythm
   my given flows are driven snow
       to slowly show how I'm living

and it's a given everything I say
is what I know   so

the beat's set   but I've got no shoes
on my feet yet and
I've not touched down
on the street yet so
I pull on my clothes
                and gone

walk to the rhythm
as it beats in my bones
weave between the streets of people
            as they're speaking into phones and oh
            there it comes
            the beginning of a lyric
                    like a miracle in miniature
                    tiptoeing to my tongue

so I speak it
trim syllables down
and repeat it
to the beat it's
got a sweet fit
and pretty soon
it feels like   I breathe it

I'm in my stride
eyes wide
I feel alive   people are stepping to the side
they can see I'm on a mission

I've got a vision of my verse
and it feels right
I must rehearse till it feels tight
and   hold on   who's calling my name?

it's Michael

I bump into him every now and again
we've not been tight
since we were ten but he somehow feels
we're the best of friends

man's cool   he left school
          and went the thug road
          no paper to hold
        - so he dug holes
          did fourteen months
          on a drug load
we press palms
his dress garms: Armani head to foot
these days never short
of bread to cut   but
my mind's on my rhyme
so I keep it shut

he's always telling me
just get together with two grand
in a month he could make me
a few grand   I'll be steppin'
          on road like a new man

Get it, wash it, cut it, push it
any competition just rush it
cos you have to save yourself

we go way back, we're brothers
what do ya say?

I just smile and try to explain
it's not my way   and that's OK
cos true say
truth be told
I think he wishes it wasn't his but
a man's business is his business
              and I've been busy with mine
              since I chose it

I switch pace and it seems strange
how people and faces change
while places stay the same
and a man says he knows you
just cos he knows your name

some people don't like change
they want routine
              not a new scheme
                    and if you seem
                          to have a new dream
                                they say *he's changed*
                                like it's some sort of
                                negative

my energy flows
making enemies
out of those who suppose
the path I chose delivering flows
just goes to show I'm a loser

just cos I choose to remove
blues through tunes
and manoeuvre yous through grooves
that can soothe any moods of doom
and have you moving shoes
through computer music
my voice is a tool and I use it
this is my path and I choose it

I'm not walking   I'm cruising
and
hold on a sec   shit
         yep
                 it's her

Gemma
my one-time dilemma
from back in the day
we used to say we'd last forever
but
you say a lot of shit
       when you're sixteen

two years older   than me and
        back then that was a lot
and she was hot
       let's just say
she taught me a lesson I never
forgot

we used to hang out
in her bedroom and get high
listen to *Ready to Die*
then one night
she got this look in her eye
surprise surprise
             till I die
I won't forget what happened next
a few new boxes got checked
and walking home
I thought

I'd become a man
         we made plans   she was training
to be a nurse
I was going away to study   plus

I'd started penning a verse

we'd talk on the phone
I'd tape my flows and send
them home
she'd have a moan
         about being alone
and over the months
I felt a change in her tone

I came home that summer
everything was weird
what we had had disappeared
and there would've been tears but   man the girl turned
cold

she kept on asking me
when would I make some dough
she wanted her man to provide stuff
I was like woah   I'm eighteen
                 and you're twenty

we had plenty of rows that were mainly
her shouting
doubting my ambition and pouting
saying
only party rhymes will ever get heard

She used to say   *there's no money*
                        in spoken word
I said *there's no money*
        in breathing either   but
                            I guess she never heard

cos I'm stood here with her now
and she's still talking
I'm still wishing
I could keep walking
        don't get me wrong it's not a hate thing
it's just boring

   that's just how it is now
this is the way   I wanna live now
                        I've got something to give now

and I don't give a shit what anyone thinks
they're living for Friday-night drinks
and designer jeans
while living inside my mind I scheme
the perfect rhyme
to shine in beams
and
        before I know it
            the rhyme builds itself and I'm done
            have to get on the phone to friends

and let them know that I soon come
cos it's   2006
and beats arrive by email

and these tales
are just the way I live

it's how I live

SPIN THE BOTTLE

Who shot ya?

I'm in a wardrobe
my torso no more
than one and a half feet
from another torso
that other torso
being female
and way more advanced
than mine

Gemma McBride
she smells like   CK One
                              and Flumps
I can't see her
in the dark
but even so
my body
still wants
to try and hide

through the scalpel-cut
crack between the doors
I can hear from outside
the start of track eighteen
on my CD of Biggie Smalls's
Ready to Die
and I am
I mean

at this exact moment in time
I would happily die
happily
pucker my lips
to the vision
of an eighteen-tonne wrecking ball
swinging through the side of this house
to flatten my life
hands stapled to my sides
palms greased
with a sheen of puberty's nerves
not moving an inch
conscious any flinch
could be taken
as a green light for action
my whole body
     in a strange awake
     yet comatose state
     of self-imposed traction

I can hear sweat trickling down your cheek
Your heartbeat sound like Sasquatch feet

shut up   Biggie!
you're not helping
     my skeleton's melting and
I'm sweating
like Roland from Grange Hill
doing a bleep test
  toe to toe
in the dark
my mind

147

flashes back
to three minutes previous

And I'm Crooklyn's finest
You rewind this, Bad Boy's behind this

shut up Biggie!

It was like *The Deer Hunter*
     watching the empty Lucozade bottle spin
on the thin 1970s throwback carpet
I imagined
Christopher Walken's wide eyes
gun barrel pressed
against my temple
     she did it gentle
on purpose
and as her wrist sent it   turning
she cut me a look
she didn't even try and hide

    It's me and you, sunshine

there were nine of us
boys four
girls five
and everybody knew
the only boy's mouth
she hadn't already
explored
with her tongue
was mine

I scanned the circle
        everybody else was on it
fourteen-year-old veterans
their eyes glaring at the bottle
pointing at me
    a sheep on his knees with hyenas
and she didn't even look
she didn't need to
she knew
    like all good strikers
the goal doesn't move
just keep your eye on the ball
it's yours
you own it

everybody's face
turned to me
in slow motion
there was no air

now there's no air   in here
I'm breathing in
what she's breathing out
I'm a horror-film victim
struck silent with a need to shout

You'll die slow but calm

shut   up   Biggie!

Who's Biggie?   her voice stabs me

outside the doors
they're counting down
to when the track's done
we step out
and Gemma pronounces
how she's 'had me'
but
I don't wanna be 'had'
      I'm not ready for this and besides
      I'm kinda into that girl in my maths class

Psst, can't we just not, Gemma, and say that we did?
      What, are you kidding?
No, I'm just, I'm just . . .
      You're just frigid!
Gemma, I don't want to –

and that's when it came
from the warm grey of the dark
the eighteen-tonne wrecking-ball fist
etched with letters spelling my name

now
      as anybody who's ever been punched fully
      in the stomach
      while standing in a cramped wardrobe
            in the dark when you're not expecting it
            and subsequently fallen out
            of said wardrobe into a crumpled heap
            in front of seven expectant 'friends'
            to a backdrop of the outro of track eighteen

from my CD of Biggie Smalls's
Ready to Die will know

there's not much you can do

I just lay there
concave
gut crushed
lungs bust
circled by amazed faces
praying for something
   anything
    to save me

but all I heard was Biggie Smalls say

Who shot ya?

WHEEL OF FORTUNE

They will not carry me in pine
they will scatter me
on the front doorstep
of the first kid back at school
who ever battered me
I take a pinch of salt with flattery
because whose line is it anyway?   Tony Slattery

something had to be done
so I did it
now I wish there were
sixty-one seconds in every minute
to-do list never finished
in this mind where ideas rise to the top
like the bubbles inside a Guinness
I will not know my limits
that might be the difference
between simply existing
and really living
          there is no prison like opinion
          given by two ears who won't listen
          you don't need eyes for vision
          see
I could write five tunes   decent
rinse them every night to a crowd full of unknown people
and if one of those people is seen to carry weight
and speaks in a magazine
a few more people are gonna believe them

please
who you dealing with?

I am not that creature
I'd rather cut my own left ear off
than suffer these eejits
so much made with no reason
I'm trying to leave a shape in the snow
like a paw before leaving
   wheel of fortune spun
   needle stuck between humdrum
   and one more tune done

I pass people in the street
and wonder how many feel
completely controlled by a beat
think we win once   so we're told to repeat
but no matter who you know
we're all alone in defeat

so I take stock   like an OXO thief

when I was young I used to wish I was a polar-bear ninja
master of the shuriken   nunchucks and sabre
now I'm older   and more comfortable with danger
sometimes I still wish
I was a polar-bear ninja

Polarbear in Conversation with Kayo Chingonyi

Kayo Chingonyi: So, I guess the first thing, in terms of context and getting a sense of where this journey begins for you, is thinking about early life and family. You mention a lot of storytellers. Can you say something about that?

Polarbear: I grew up in the house that was always full. Up until I was like eleven, when people moved back home, there was at least my two grandparents living with us. For a good couple of years it was my auntie, uncle and three cousins too, all of us in the same house. So, it was a kind of constant talk. There weren't that many books. No one was anti academia – quite the opposite, in fact – but there just, it wasn't like, a thing. People were working, and then when they weren't working, they were chilling, and chilling meant eating and music and sharing stories in the kitchen.

Like, the kitchen was a station. So whenever you'd— I'd get home from school or in the morning, there'll just be people there: family, friends who come through the back entry between the houses. My nan, when she first came, she'd managed to get a place from the council, so she had lodgers, so people who were arriving would stay in my nan's house... And that relationship kind of just carried on when they got their own places everyone just came to where she was, so there was just a constant stream of characters, and loads of stories – stories about journeys, getting here and then just navigating, navigating being here.

KC: Mm.

P: And whether that'd be the Jamaican side or the Irish side, it was like, it was just constant, man. And, you know, they would get retold, and looking back now, in hindsight, they would often get refined as well. I would hear the same thing, and it would be slightly different, or slightly more, like, on point, or maybe even exaggerated a little. And seeing how some people would be more listeners, and then the other ones who would do the talking and just hold court. My nan being the kinda pinnacle of that, that role. Just like, campfire business. It was one of them.

KC: That reminds me of a way you used to describe what you do, which I think was even the name of your first recording of poems together, 'Just Talking'.

P: Before we recorded it, man. Yeah, it was.

KC: Back in Myspace days.

P: Yeah, for sure, man. [inaudible]

KC: I'm interested in the qualification you made back then. It *is* just talking, but then there's a crafted element as well. And where does that early kind of immersion in stories meet with craft? What was your first exposure to the craft of storytelling, putting together words?

P: It was music, I guess, like a lot of people. And not just hip hop, but before that as well, you know? Lyrics, it was lyrics, and it was, it was statements. This chorus, or that phrase, certain lines that kinda jumped out. It was in Depeche Mode's, 'Enjoy the Silence' as much as it was in 'Buffalo Soldier' or something. Sometimes it was an image, other times it was just the way words sounded, nothing to do with meaning, just listening, and pictures arising in my mind. It just charged you up, like when Nan or family, when they were telling stories, it all sort of felt like it was about them, being there, in the moment. I was listening and picturing things, but really what I was hypnotized by was the magic of it, them there, no bells or whistles, just feeling present and connected.

I'd always written stories since young, but I first started rhyming when – I guess like year eight, really? Like, year seven, year eight. But because we'd moved house at that point and I was by myself and my school was just, it was mostly

English – it always used to be a joke – school was Oasis, and home was De La Soul. It was one of them ones. I'd dress one way with school people and completely different round my old mates and family. And not that either one was better, but I definitely felt more ease at home and around my people I grew up with, but, you know, the Oasis, all that shit, that had its merits as well.

It was just that idea of words together and the flow of things, the patterns, and enjoying that. It wasn't conscious at the time, but in hindsight, there is that thing of just knowing how much is enough and, not just economy, but like, the choices of it, that I'd grown up around and was unconsciously studying. The choice of space, when to make sure people knew, or when to allow for that sense of ambiguity. Nan was a master magician with it because it felt like it wasn't over until she said it was over, and then when she said it was over, it couldn't have been over at any other time. It just felt... Do you know what I mean? And then it'd be time to eat, which is just magic on top of magic, right? There'd always be music in the background too, whether from another room or from the little shitty radio or something. The layers of it, all the references bleeding into each other. Magic. And the older I've got, the more it feels like magic, and I just feel more and more proud and appreciative the more I think about it.

KC: Mm.

P: I didn't even answer the question did I? The reason I called the thing 'Just Talking', is, partly, was a kinda tongue-in-cheek comment on a thing that my friend had said when I started to get a bit of a name, he was like, 'It's just talking,' just to keep my feet on the ground and that, to calm me down like we do in Brum. But then there were people I met later, who used it in a more spiky and derogatory way, where it was like, spoken word to them seemed less crafted or more thrown together than something that's on the page, for example, kind of giving them the finger— I always hoped that people who really listened and had an ear for the craft and music of it would know and go, ah, it's more than that.

KC: Yeah. So through your teens, you're like writing, maybe making tapes and spitting over beats.

P: M-hmm.

KC: But also having the kind of lyricism, for want of a better word, of British music at the time. Brit-pop and that kinda thing, as I remember it, it had a kind of attitude to it, a no-nonsense kind of approach—

P: Yeah. For sure.

KC: I think it's there in your work. I guess as well in some of the stuff, like, Mike Skinner initially put out, in terms a particularly British way of doing things, which is no-frills—

P: Yeah. I can see that.

KC: Just as much as you need to get across the thing.

P: Completely. And also I would argue that even in those no frills things there was a hope, and whether that's my own projection or investment over time or whatever, it just felt like it inherently – and you know, New Labour and all that stuff before it got exposed – it was like, there was a real sense of people just doing things for themselves, like when mates were in bands and whatever. Get to the point, do it well, share it.

Me and my lot never had aspirations to be in a band or on stage, it was just something that we liked doing. Then what became clear by the time I get to, like, sixth-form age, was like, well, the Oasis lot from school who, you know, I was cool with and everything, but the divide started happening in terms of sensibility. They were all like, you know, beers and bouncing up and down and Loaded magazine, and that just... it wasn't me at all, do you know what I mean?

Plus, as well, my first serious romantic relationship had started at sixth-form, and that changed everything. Completely. Cos that was like, right, well, yo, I don't have to be a role-play version of myself — I can just be me, into what I'm into, and hang out with somebody who's cool, and into stuff too and there's music, and books and films and sharing stuff and I started to feel the urge to express what I was thinking and feeling. That's when I first started writing letters, or things that were meant for somebody else, you know? For her. Rhyming was always like, mine, and up until then it was mostly just to feel cool, or to seem cool, or to get responses from people I respected. To go like, 'yeah, alright, nice one Stevey, that's sick, whatever that is'. But the first, the first incarnation of me actually wanting to communicate things that I felt or thought and to open up, were those initial letters to my girlfriend, you know?

KC: Mm.

P: I kind of withdrew from both social camps at that point. Basically I was swerving the boys, especially in any kind of group cos it was like, yo, just me and her, this is what I'm supposed to be, just being with somebody and communicating and having conversations about stuff, you know? The rest can do one. That's when reading properly kicked in too, I reckon by the second year of A-level—

KC: Mm.

P: I was also feeling more and more conscious about where I was from and the culture I'd grown up with. A lot of family had moved back to Jamaica or away and I was really missing it, and I was really proud, but I was also really in a sort of strange situation, because I don't look like what I'm from as well, you know? Nobody would know just to look at me. So it's that weird thing where I was kinda navigating – I guess, I don't wanna say what I'm allowed to be, but kind of what I'm allowed to be and celebrate, you know? I'd felt a lot of other people telling me who I am and who I'm not. And so I, that's when I started writing stories and creating characters. I think I was just trying to figure things out... find my place, but even then it always felt like I was trying to celebrate my upbringing, the characters, the traits and things that I loved.

KC: So are the characters like a mask? You know, like at carnival.

P: I'm not sure. Possibly. That's a thing isn't it?

KC: You put on the jolly sailor and that is an exploration of that part of yourself made big.

P: Yeah. And just running with what felt right. I wasn't even sure what I was doing, but what was lovely about writing the letters, and later the spoken word pieces, was they felt like these moments that I wanted to share. I remember being more and more conscious of homage, it being like, this is what Uncle Lenny and Nan used to do in the kitchen and thinking: what if I can do that, just hold people like they did, figuratively speaking – that becoming an exciting idea. But again, performance was not even on the radar. Genuinely, not on the radar, in terms of public performance as such, or a stage.

KC: I feel you.

P: Partly because I wasn't aware that anything like that happened. No one in my family was on stage – but they held court. Do you know what I mean? There weren't performance aspirations. My granddad's brother was a singer, a club singer, and that set up some amazing and messed up stories about him and his brother going round to places and singing in venues where they weren't even allowed to drink in the bar, but it was the story that mattered. Do you know what I mean? So you'd have these kind of gorgeous perspectives on kinda messed up stuff, but told with such warmth and ownership, that it was like, I don't know, man. I don't know, I just loved the idea of kinda keeping that going somehow.

I'm not really good at telling jokes, but whenever I would relay stuff... I remember I started making stuff up and bending the truth, and just creating things to have something to say, to feel what that felt like, trying to hold court with a story. Just enjoying the sense of holding people's attention, I guess.

KC: You've mentioned a few things I wanna pick up on, one of them being this idea of having a foot in both camps in one sense.

P: Yeah.

KC: The Irish side, the Jamaican side, growing up when you did in Birmingham... National Front was a definite issue. And National Front weren't really feeling the Irish side or the Jamaican side. But then someone might look at you and make an assumption: this person is from such and such.

P: Yeah.

KC: It's such a fascinating aspect of growing up, especially in the UK. If someone doesn't have a language for where you're from or where you fit, it's a proper confusion. And it can't be okay until they work it out.

P: Completely. It's very different now, but between my mid-teens to, I'd say, mid-twenties, there was a real anger and frustration in me – and also maybe an overcompensation in different situations: making sure that people knew, because people thinking I'm just white – which I think people were thinking as default – was my worst-case scenario.

Or even being associated with that straight Englishness and it feeling wrong— And just retreating and retreating, and social circles getting smaller and smaller just to avoid it. And that sometimes being racial or cultural, sometimes being gender. It's a weird thing. My nan would say, the best ducks can swim in any pond. But you go like, right, okay, that feels like a strength, but none of these different ponds make me feel completely at ease. Do you know what I mean? And then you go to uni, and see the levels of dough and that's a whole extra layer to unpick Cos you go, oh right, we're poor! Shit. I didn't realise.

And I think navigating those things of – maybe having children changed it slightly too – but I still feel that there are certain voices and certain personalities whose validation or praise or acknowledgement I value way more than others, and that comes directly from growing up, you know? And how different home was behind that front door. Like, home being an island. And sometimes literally. Because there are people in my family who were actually told they were coming home when they arrived, so they kind of owned the empire, by default, in the kind of way that their kids, our parents and then us, were like, what the hell are you doing? Like, why are there coronation plates on the wall? But to them, they wouldn't shake that pride till they died, man. They wouldn't even acknowledge they'd been undermined out loud for thirty, forty years.

And I feel now what's nice is I'm past the point of necessarily needing people to know I come from a mixed heritage. I still like it when it's registered or acknowledged, and hopefully through everything – whether it be the novels, or whether it be the short pieces – these things are in there. Do you know what I mean? I feel a little bit more sure in myself these days, as opposed to being almost apologetic sometimes.

KC: Yeah. Apologetic or like, there's that double consciousness, the need to defend a particular position.

P: Exactly.

KC: Cos you've been forced into—

P: Yep.

KC: —a side or whatever.

P: Completely. And there's certain situations sometimes where you're like, you overstep that, and you're defending something that you don't need to— and also, you maybe shouldn't really be doing. And then you can end up... It's a weird dance, man.

I've been talking about this a lot with my mom. Just about her experiences in Birmingham growing up as second generation back then, and just trying to navigate it through to motherhood and then raising kids who are navigating an ever-so-slightly filtered version of that same reality.

We were joking. I was just like, right, if I'm in a supermarket – this is gonna sound creepy now – if I'm in the supermarket, and I've got my basket, and I hear – and my radar is sharp at this point – if I hear an older – and I'm not talking Caribbean, I mean specifically an older female Jamaican voice – I will gladly pretend to be shopping for ages just to walk and listen, because that is pretty much the warmest and the most comforting sound and voice to me, and that I miss so truly.

And I wanna pay homage to that, but I also don't wanna share it, cos it feels like mine. So it's that weird navigation of like, how do you communicate to people without broadcasting it as if you're trying to get points or something for having, you know, this gift of heritage. Do you know what I mean? It's a very strange dance. And I guess the lovely thing about writing a piece or hearing somebody I respect, like you, say it comes through in the references, hopefully what that means is I got that balance right. It was enough to flag in the mind of somebody who has their own version of that othered experience, but it wasn't too much that it was spoon-feeding or broadcasting something for its own sake.

KC: How do you know how much to leave in and how much to take out of a piece?

P: I really don't know – I should ask you exactly the same question. It's a feeling, isn't it? You have to own these sounds you make and trust your gut. I do know that a massive aid in that respect is the mouth. How something feels on my tongue.

KC: Hmm.

P: You write something on the page – I do, anyway – I write something on the page and I'm just not sure whether it's right or feels right, but as soon as I speak something out loud... What's wrong feels wrong very quickly.

I used to get really hyped off of using specific patterns that somebody listening who's into rhyming might know is a homage to a particular DOOM verse on a particular DOOM track. I think the same thing applies. You do it too much, it becomes self-congratulatory and pretentious. You do just enough— And it's always less, isn't it? It's always less.

KC: Yeah.

P: Always less. That's a good title.

KC: I have that problem with, um, Chester P metaphors.

P: Yeah.

KC: Like there's one from *Music From the Corner* – 'Some drown in the depths of the night's dark river' – which I've queried in my work. I'm not certain anybody's spotted that.

P: Some things hide. Like treasure.

KC: It's for me, but it's also being shared, and I'm keeping a certain boundary that means—

P: Exactly. For the real listeners, but that's it, right? That—

KC: —only the people who need to know will know.

COMPOSITION NOTES

HEARTBURN (2009)
- on the walk back from Southbank to Kentish

SAGAT (2005)
- on a building site in Perry Barr

ALEXANDER THE GRAPE (2006)
- on a battered futon on Islip St

BROKEN (2005)
- in Mom's spare room

DANNY (2006)
- on the train to a school visit in Bradford

DAVID (2004)
- on the 140 bus to a guitar loop from Andy

DEATH-PROOF (2008)
- chopping carrots, listening to a Lenstrumental

FINGERS (2005)
- in my teenage bedroom by moonlight

CREATURES OF HABIT (2008)
- in MAP Café making one pot of tea last all day

FRONT STEP (2008)
- on the way up to Lichfield to see Len

INSIDE (2004)
- on a Saturday morning after, while Andy slept

JESSICA (2006)
- on the weekend I first performed it at OneTaste

COMPTON (2007)
- on the train home from seeing my sister

MOVES (2008)
- to my favourite instrumental ever while Len tinkered with the drum parts

repeaT (2009)
- at 2am, to a track Alex sent, rocking our youngest to sleep

SCENE (FOR DAVID J) (2008)
- coming home from a gig in East

SCOTCH (2009)
- on a long walk after a meeting with T.V. people

SEVEN THIRTY (2006)
- on Mom's living room floor to a CD Alex sent

SPIN THE BOTTLE (2008)
- for Inua's Rap Party thing

WHEEL OF FORTUNE (2009)
- on a night bus home, thinking of bigger things

IMAGE NOTES

Gillott Road View (p.xiii)
- the room where the stories first sprouted, taken
  by Andrew Roberts

Bedroom Sessions 7: Andrew (p.7)
- the music that sparked those first words, taken
  by Steven Camden

Park Road (p.13)
- two of the storytellers who inspired it all, taken
  by Patricia Woods

Brum Journeys (p.33)
- post-gig thoughts and ideas, taken by Andrew
Roberts

4 a.m. Chats (p.39)
- writing without paper, taken by Andrew Roberts

On the Way (p.51)
- heading to an early gig, taken by Andrew Roberts

Brutalism (p.55)
- old writing spot, taken by Steven Camden

Station (p.59)
- coming home, taken by Andrew Roberts

Dons (p.71)
- capturing heroes (David J + Stickman) on my first
ever tour, taken by Steven Camden

No Sleep (p.77)
- I write while Andy makes, taken by
  Steven Camden

Drop Foot (p. 91)
- dancing with Tuffy sparked plenty ideas, taken by Andrew Roberts

On the Wall (p. 101)
- comes with me wherever I go, taken by Steven Camden

Bedroom Sessions 18: Me and Len (p. 103)
- sock over the Woolworths mic, taken by Andrew Roberts

Company Ideas (p. 111)
- using the art to try and make an impact, taken by Steven Camden

Early Drafts (p. 117)
- scribbled schemes that became something, taken by Steven Camden

Festival Gents (p. 125)
- me, Inua Ellams and Byron Vincent, taken by Rakesh Parmar

Deal Real (p. 133)
- rhyming on hallowed turf, taken by Olly Grove

Archive (p. 136)
- childhood recording nobody will ever hear, taken by Steven Camden

Logo (p. 139)
- created by Pete Wilson a.k.a. GOONISM

Cali (p. 145)
- early days, taken by Steven Camden (on timer)

Hanover, Jamaica (p. 153)
- writing with Granddad, taken by Steven Camden

Zone (p. 157)
- these days, taken by Yael Shavit

Acknowledgements

Thank you:
Kayo for reaching out
My family and friends for inspiration
and support
Birmingham for the fight
Anybody who's ever really listened

I was raised by storytellers
Now I'm raising storytellers
them ones

As I created the pieces collected in *The Lost Chronicle*, they always felt like short films to me. Sequences of scenes with chosen shots, cuts and edits that would play in my mind as I spoke them out loud. Each of those films had its own soundtrack and score, provided by the amazing musical artists I grew up listening to. Several of the pieces reference specific lyrics in grateful acknowledgment to their creators for their inspiration and influence on my work, and in celebration of their impact on my life. Thank you.

Epigraph

One of the biggest influences on my spoken words, pattern- and rhythm-wise. I could've listed so many amazing lines, but this album genuinely felt like a soundtrack to me finding my own voice, and these line in particular became a kind of private mantra. Rest in peace.

'Is he still a fly guy clappin' if nobody ain't hear it? And can they testify from inner spirit?'
– MF DOOM, 'Accordion', *Madvillainy* (2004)

David

I can remember the first time we heard it: in the back of Andy's mom's car driving past Thimblemill swimming baths, and us looking at each like, *What the hell?* The Hammer Shuffle was learned pronto.

'Hammer Time!'
– MC Hammer, 'U Can't Touch This' (single version, 1990)

Creatures of Habit

When this album dropped it felt like the world shifted. So many new characters all at once. I remember, even then, smiling at the juxtaposition of kung-fu- and geometry-laced lyrics from Staten Island being bumped through Walkman headphones on the 140 bus in Rowley Regis. You had to pick a favourite, and mine was always Johnny Blaze.

'Hey, you, get off my cloud
You don't know me and you don't know my
style... '
– Wu-Tang Clan, 'Method Man', *Enter The Wu-Tang (36 Chambers)* (1993)

Compton
This album was the physical incarnation of rebellion for me. First time I heard it on a copied cassette from my older cousins, I was so terrified of my mom's response to me having it that I took it to the park, unspooled the entire tape, snapped the cassette and threw it in a bush, just to be sure she'd never find it. Even then, knowing it was there in the park kept me awake at night. That sense of rebellion and channelled anger would definitely become a big part of my life and serve as fuel for my creativity.

'So when I'm in your neighbourhood, you'd better duck!
Cos Ice Cube is crazy as fuck!
As I leave, believe I'm stompin'
But when I come back, boy, I'm coming straight outta Compton'
– N.W.A., 'Straight Outta Compton', *Straight Outta Compton* (1988)

Spin the Bottle
Biggie Smalls's music seemed to be the background soundtrack for multiple seminal moments in my life. The tone of his voice over '80s

soul samples as a score through house party speakers, car stereos and boom boxes is attached to the short films of my memories and always seemed to fit moments perfectly. I wanted to celebrate that with this piece.

'Who shot ya?'
'I can hear sweat trickling down your cheek
Your heartbeat sound like Sasquatch feet'
'And I'm Crooklyn's finest
You rewind this, Bad Boy's behind this'
'You'll die slow but calm'
– The Notorious B.I.G., 'Who Shot Ya?', *Big Poppa/Warning* (reissue, 1995)

A Note on the Author

Steven Camden (Polarbear) is one of the most respected spoken word artists in the UK. He has graced stages from Kuala Lumpur to California via Glastonbury and the Royal Shakespeare Company. His work has featured on BBC Radio 1, 3 and 6. Steven has written three young adult novels for HarperCollins: *Tape*; *It's About Love* and *Nobody Real*. His poetry collection for children, *Everything All At Once,* won the 2019 CLPE Award. *The Lost Chronicle* is the first book to collect his spoken-word pieces for adults.

A Note on the Type

Warnock is a serif typeface designed by Robert Slimbach. The design features sharp, wedge-shaped serifs. The typeface is named after John Warnock, one of the co-founders of Adobe. John Warnock's son, Chris Warnock, requested that Slimbach design the typeface as a tribute to his father in 1997. It was later released as a commercial font by Adobe in 2000 under the name Warnock Pro.

April

Music for the Dead and Resurrected
by Valzhyna Mort

Music for the Dead and Resurrected captures the complexity of living in the shadows of imperial force, of the vulnerability of bodies, of seeing with more than one's eyes.

Valzhyna Mort's work is characterised by a memorial sensibility that honours those lost to the violences of nation states. In *Music for the Dead and Resurrected* the poet offers us a body of work which balances political import with serious play. There are few poets writing with such an intuitive sense of the balance between arcane and contemporary currents in poetry. Mort's lines are timeless, finely honed to last beyond a single lifetime.

June

Sonnets for Albert by Anthony Joseph

With *Sonnets for Albert*, Anthony Joseph returns to the autobiographical material explored in his earlier collection *Bird Head Son*. In this followup he weighs the impact of being the son of an absent, or mostly absent father, in poems that, though they threaten to break under the weight of their emotions, are always masterfully poised as the stylish man they depict.

October

A Little Resurrection by Selina Nwulu

A Little Resurrection, the debut full-length collection of Selina Nwulu, is the work of a questing sensibility. These poems are equally at home in the golden light of Senegal as they are in the harsh winds of Yorkshire. In these poems blackness itself is complicated, extending the resonances of being to reflect the self in a state of flux, a fugitive spirit battling the harm of erasure. There is a profound joy in these poems, all the more powerful for being hard-won. This book heralds the branching out of an important trajectory in Anglophone poetry.

November

The Lost Chronicle: 2004–2009 by Polarbear

Polarbear is one of the most influential poets of his generation. The work collected here is the work that made his name. These poems have racked up hundreds of thousands of views online, lodging themselves in the hearts and minds of readers and audiences alike. His particular gift is for the many kinds of music a line can contain. He marries the intricate, compulsive, rhyming strategies of rap with the schanachie's gift for telling a story and the saxophonist's flair for bending the possibilities of sound.